THE UK

KU-090-032

BY

ROBIN TWIDDY

BookLife
PUBLISHING

©2019
BookLife Publishing Ltd.
King's Lynn
Norfolk PE30 4LS
All rights reserved.
Printed in Malaysia.

A catalogue record for this
book is available from the
British Library.

ISBN: 978-1-78637-688-6

Written by:
Robin Twiddy

Edited by:
John Wood

Designed by:
Gareth Liddington

Photocredits:

Cover – Lipowski Milan, Pavlo Lys, Iryna Kashpur, Alexey Fedorenko, piyaphong, Kiev. Vector, Alinute Silzeviciute, Claudio Divizia, 4 – Alinute Silvezeviciute, Tanarch, Satori Studio, 5 – Lorna Roberts, Richie Chan, ArtMari, 6 – littlewormy, Anna Jastrzebska, Paolo Trovo, Quang Ho, satit sewtiw, 8 – aslysun, Paolo Trovo, Akvaartist, 9 – Ollie Taylor, sarayut jun-ngam, 10 – XXLPhoto, Mykhailo Brodskyi, Suti Stock Photo, 11 – ian woolcock, Padmayogini, 12 – pim pic, comzeal images, FreshStock, 13 – Peter Nadolski, David Berry, 14 – andersphoto, Steve Bramall, CO Leong, 15 – xpixel, Fedorov Oleksiy, WDG Photo, ArtMari, 16 – MaraZe, GreenArt, EddieCloud, Richard Bradford, Billion Photos, 17 – Eloise Adler, larik_malasha, 18 – D. Pimborough, vulcano, peresanz, KateChe, 19 – Lars Poyansky, Creative Photo Corner, Thomas Holt, Billy Stock, FILINmore, 20 – S-F, Lucky Team Studio, 21 – VanderWolf Images, thidanphon taoha, Nieuwland Photography, Claudio Divizia, snapgalleria, 22 – Stephen Gibson, Joe Gough, Thomas Bethge, Alberto Masnovo, 23 – chrisdorney, Paul Daniels, Natata, Purple Anvil, 24 – Dave Head, Paper Street Design, 25 – David Winn Photography, Kevin Eaves, NV Group Studio, 26 – Pelin Oleg and Nathalia, Jule_Berlin, ArtMari, 27 – Dark_Side, CKP1001, Kelenart, 28 – Syda Productions, 30 – Anna_Pustynnikova, norikko.
Images are courtesy of Shutterstock.com. With thanks to Getty Images, Thinkstock Photo and iStockphoto.

All facts, statistics, web addresses and URLs in this book were verified as valid and accurate at time of writing.
No responsibility for any changes to external websites or references can be accepted by either the author or publisher.

CONTENTS

CATCH UNDERGRO
TO LEICE
SQUARE

THINGS TO
• LONDON
• BUCKIN
• OLYMP

Words that look like <u>this</u> can be found in the glossary on page 31.

Special Express

SINGLE

Number: 1666
Train: 704
Seat: 12B

TRAIN COMPANY

TRAIN TICKET

SINGLE

WELCOME TO THE UK

Hello, my name is Katie. I live in Cornwall in the UK with my family. We are going to take a road trip and see as much of the country as we can.

I NEED TO PLAN OUR JOURNEY VERY CAREFULLY TO MAKE SURE WE GET TO SEE AS MUCH OF THIS BEAUTIFUL COUNTRY AS POSSIBLE.

THE UK IS MADE UP OF COUNTIES. EACH ONE HAS ITS OWN NAME, HISTORY AND SPECIAL TYPES OF FOOD. WE ARE GOING TO VISIT AS MANY OF THEM AS WE CAN.

NORTHERN IRELAND

SCOTLAND

ENGLAND

WALES

The UK is short for the United Kingdom. It is a very interesting place to live. It is made up of four countries: England, Scotland, Wales and Northern Ireland. Each country in the United Kingdom has its own <u>culture</u> and history, but they also have a lot in common.

THE MONARCHY

Although she doesn't rule the country, we do have a queen and a royal family. The Queen is called Elizabeth the Second. The royal family have palaces, castles and homes all around the country. Maybe we will see one on our journey.

UNITED KINGD
GREAT BRIT
AND NORTHERN I

PASSPORT

GOVERNMENT

The UK is run by the government and not by the royal family. The government is a group of people that make the laws and decide how the country works.

THESE ARE THE HOUSES OF PARLIAMENT, WHERE THE GOVERNMENT MEETS AND RUNS THE COUNTRY FROM.

Look out for coordinates in boxes like these. Use the internet to explore these places online. You can ask an adult to help you.

THE EDEN PROJECT

The Eden Project is one of my favourite places in the country. It includes lots of big domes that work like greenhouses. It means that you can visit a <u>rainforest</u> in the UK.

I HAVE NEVER SEEN SO MANY PLANTS BEFORE!

WHAT IS AT THE EDEN PROJECT?

There is so much to see here. There is the rainforest <u>biome</u>, the Mediterranean biome and lots of outdoor activities such as zip-lining and climbing. You can also buy food grown in the biomes.

THE EDEN PROJECT IS REALLY FUN - I CAN'T WAIT TO SEE WHAT THE REST OF THE COUNTRY HAS IN STORE FOR US.

THE JOURNEY BEGINS IN THE SOUTH

The Eden Project is in Cornwall. Cornwall is the most southern point of the UK. It is the closest part of the country to the <u>Equator</u>. This means that it is usually warmer than other parts of the UK.

CORNWALL HAS BEACHES THAT ARE FAMOUS FOR SURFING.

CORNISH AND THE CELTS

People in Cornwall speak English, but it is one of the few places in the UK that still has its own <u>ancient</u> language, Cornish. This was the language spoken by their Celtic <u>ancestors</u>.

IN <u>FOLKLORE</u>, IT IS SAID THAT GIANTS ROAMED THE CORNISH COUNTRYSIDE AND HELPED TO SHAPE THE LANDSCAPE.

STONEHENGE

Stonehenge was really amazing. It is believed that it was built over 5,000 years ago. People come from all around the world to see the famous stone circle.

PEOPLE STILL GATHER AT STONEHENGE TO CELEBRATE THE <u>SUMMER SOLSTICE</u>. IT LOOKS LIKE FUN.

THE MYSTERY OF STONEHENGE

Nobody knows for sure how the people of <u>prehistoric</u> Britain moved those giant stones, or what they were used for. Some people believe that they were used for religious reasons.

SOMERSET AND WILTSHIRE

THE SOMERSET LEVELS

SOMERSET

Stonehenge is in Wiltshire. Wiltshire is next to Somerset, which is in the south-west of England. Somerset has lots of beautiful countryside including hills, flatlands and coastline. Travelling across Somerset, you can find parts of the country's history, from castles to Stone Age burial sites.

BATH

We visited the city of Bath in Somerset. It is named after the Roman-built baths that the city is famous for. The water is still heated by natural <u>hot springs</u> just as it was when the Romans first built it in <u>AD</u> 75.

THE BATH WAS REALLY GREAT, BUT THEY WON'T LET YOU SWIM IN IT BECAUSE OF THE <u>ALGAE</u>.

ROMAN BATH IN BATH, SOMERSET

THE WHITE CLIFFS OF DOVER

Next, we visited Dover and the famous white cliffs in Kent. The cliffs are white because they are made of chalk. The cliffs reach a height of 106 metres.

THE CLIFFS ARE EVEN WHITER THAN I THOUGHT THEY WOULD BE.

Travellers returning from Europe by sea would know that they were almost home when they could see the famous white cliffs. The largest castle in England sits on top of the cliffs. It was started by William the Conqueror in AD 1066.

KENT

Canterbury is also in Kent – it is one of the most famous historic cities in the UK. When we visited, we went to see the cathedral. People have been travelling to the cathedral from all around the world since medieval times.

THESE JOURNEYS TO CANTERBURY CATHEDRAL, AND OTHER JOURNEYS LIKE THEM, ARE CALLED PILGRIMAGES.

The cathedral was built in around AD 600 by St Augustine. It helped to make Kent the first Anglo-Saxon kingdom to follow Christianity.

WE THEN STOPPED OFF AT THE WHITSTABLE OYSTER FESTIVAL. THE PARADE WAS FUN, BUT I DON'T THINK I LIKE OYSTERS!

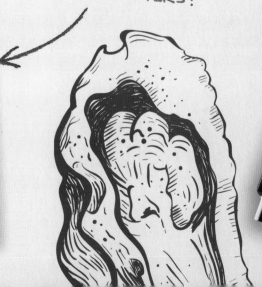

TRAIN TICKET
SINGLE
TRAIN COMPANY
SINGLE
Number: 1666
Train: 704

BIG BEN

Wow, there is so much to see in London. It is the capital city of England and is home to lots of famous landmarks such as the Houses of Parliament, Buckingham Palace, the Natural History Museum and much more.

I think I am most excited about seeing Big Ben. It is probably the most famous clock in the world. Big Ben is actually the name of the biggest bell in the tower, and not the clock, but when people say Big Ben they are usually talking about the whole thing – tower, clock and bells.

A SYMBOL

The tower, clock and bells were completed in 1859, and have been a symbol of London ever since. Not only is the clock well known for being an amazing sight, but it is also well known for how accurate it is.

YOU CAN HEAR BIG BEN FROM 8 KILOMETRES AWAY. WOW!

The main bell weighs an incredible 13.7 tonnes and makes a very loud chime. It makes the musical note of E when it is struck. It is really amazing to hear in real life.

I WOULDN'T WANT TO BE IN THE TOWER WHEN THE BELLS ARE STRUCK!

SHERWOOD FOREST

There is lots to see in the Midlands, from castles to forests. But there was one forest that I really wanted to see – the famous Sherwood Forest.

SHERWOOD
FOREST
COORDINATES
53.209203,
-1.075473'

The forest is 375 <u>hectares</u> in size and is home to lots of different plants and wildlife. Deep in the forest is the legendary Major Oak. It is thought to be around 1,000 years old.

ROBIN HOOD

Sherwood Forest is home to the legend of Robin Hood. The old stories say that Robin Hood lived in this forest with his band of Merry Men. They would steal from the rich of Nottingham to give to the poor.

REAL OR NOT?

No one knows for sure if Robin Hood actually existed, or if the myth is based on lots of different outlaws. Either way, the legend is exciting and still draws people from around the world to Sherwood Forest.

I HAD LOTS OF FUN IN SHERWOOD FOREST. I JUST WISH I'D HAD TIME TO SEE NOTTINGHAM CASTLE AS WELL.

THE PEAK DISTRICT

The next stop on our journey was the Peak District. The Peak District National Park is an area of protected land covering 1,438 square kilometres. It is known for its stunning views, historic villages and amazing caves.

PEAK DISTRICT COORDINATES
53.340217,
-1.778537

We went to the Peak Cavern. When you enter the cavern, you can see where people made ropes for the local lead mines for over 400 years.

PEAK CAVERN

I REALLY ENJOYED HAVING A GO AT MAKING ROPES JUST LIKE THEY DID HUNDREDS OF YEARS AGO.

HIKING

We went hiking when we were in the Peak District. There are loads of different trails to follow. Make sure you bring your hiking boots. When you hike through the Peak District, you will see lots of wildlife and even some types of animals that can't be found anywhere else.

FOR THE LOVE OF CAKES

Derbyshire is well known for its baking. When we were in Derbyshire, there were lots of tea shops. The best thing about the tea shops is that they have homemade cakes.

I REALLY LIKED THE BAKEWELL TARTS. THEY ARE EVEN BETTER WHEN YOU EAT THEM IN BAKEWELL!

CAERNARFON CASTLE

When we visited Wales, we saw Caernarfon Castle. It is probably the most impressive castle I have ever seen. King Edward I started building the castle in 1283 to help him control the recently <u>conquered</u> Welsh people.

I did lots of fun things at the castle that really helped bring the history alive. But the most exciting was the <u>holographic</u> game that allows the player to control dragons flying around the castle.

EVEN THOUGH IT IS A REALLY IMPRESSIVE CASTLE, WELSH REBELS MANAGED TO TAKE THE CASTLE IN 1294.

WALES

Wales is one of the four countries that make up the UK. It has two main languages, English and Welsh. Wales uses the same <u>currency</u> as England, pound sterling (£).

THE WELSH FLAG HAS A DRAGON ON IT, WHICH I THINK IS REALLY COOL.

Cardiff is the capital of Wales and it is also the largest city in Wales. Wales is known as the 'land of song' and is famous for its <u>choirs</u> and solo singers.

THE GIANT'S CAUSEWAY

Northern Ireland has some amazing places to visit, such as the Giant's Causeway. It is made of around 40,000 <u>hexagonal</u> stone columns formed by a volcanic eruption 60 million years ago.

GIANT'S CAUSEWAY COORDINATES:
55.241159,
-6.511959

LEGEND OF THE GIANT'S CAUSEWAY

Legend says that a giant, Finn McCool, built the causeway to reach the other side of the water. When he got there, he found a much bigger giant. Quickly, Finn ran back and disguised himself as a baby. The other giant got scared – "If this is the size of the baby, how big must its dad be?" the giant thought, and he ran away.

I DIDN'T SEE ANY GIANTS, BUT THE CAUSEWAY WAS AMAZING.

NORTHERN IRELAND

In Northern Ireland, we also visited the Titanic Belfast. The Titanic Belfast is a museum found at the ship yard that built the Titanic.

WALKING INTO AN EXACT COPY OF A CABIN FROM THE TITANIC WAS INCREDIBLE AND REALLY MADE ME FEEL LIKE I WAS THERE.

TITANIC BELFAST

The museum tells the story of the Titanic, from its creation in Belfast right up to when it crashed into the iceberg. One of the things I really liked about the Titanic museum was how you could experience the sights and smells of the Titanic.

BLACKPOOL TOWER

Next we visited Blackpool Tower. The tower was built in 1894. It is 158 metres tall and made from 2,261 tonnes of steel, 84 tonnes of cast iron and over five million bricks.

AFTER THE TOWER, WE ATE FISH AND CHIPS ON THE PIER. THERE IS NOTHING LIKE FISH AND CHIPS BY THE SEA.

Blackpool Tower was really great. Inside we visited the circus, the indoor play area, the Blackpool Tower Dungeons, and the ballroom. Then we travelled to the top of the tower for the amazing views. It felt very high.

BLACKPOOL TOWER WAS INSPIRED BY THE EIFFEL TOWER IN PARIS, FRANCE. I THINK THEY BOTH LOOK GREAT.

LANCASHIRE

Blackpool Tower is in Lancashire. Lancashire has some amazing history and is a very <u>rural</u> area. Even though it is a rural county, it was the home of the <u>Industrial Revolution</u>. Two of the UK's most famous cities can be found in Lancashire: Manchester and Liverpool.

We had fun exploring the cities, but I was most excited about visiting Blackpool. People visit Blackpool for the Pleasure Beach, the Blackpool Illuminations and Blackpool Tower.

THIS IS LIVERPOOL

THE PLEASURE BEACH IS ONE OF THE UK'S BIGGEST THEME PARKS. IT HAS LOADS OF RIDES AND WAS SUPER FUN.

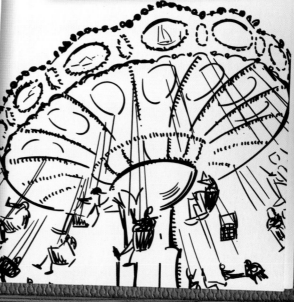

HADRIAN'S WALL

THE NORTH

Before you reach the border between England and Scotland, you will find Hadrian's Wall. This was built to mark the north-west edge of the Roman Empire.

THE WALL ISN'T VERY TALL NOW, BUT IT IS STILL PRETTY AMAZING.

It was built by the Romans on orders from the emperor Hadrian in AD 122. The wall was 4.6 metres tall in places, and 3 metres wide. It had towers and <u>barracks</u> and was guarded by Roman troops.

Hadrian's Wall goes up and down hills and must have been a breathtaking sight back then. It really shows what the ancient Romans could do. It took nearly 15,000 men roughly six years to build.

DAD WANTED TO WALK IT, BUT MUM SAID THAT IT WOULD TAKE OVER A WEEK AND WE STILL HADN'T VISITED SCOTLAND YET.

Hadrian's Wall is around 135 kilometres long. The wall runs from coast to coast and people travel from all around to walk along the famous landmark.

LOCH NESS

We finally made it to Loch Ness in Scotland. Loch means lake and there are lots of lochs in the Highlands. Loch Ness is special because of the mysterious Loch Ness Monster.

THE LOCH IS AROUND 37 KILOMETRES LONG AND IS AROUND 230 METRES DEEP IN PLACES.

THE MONSTER

People travel from all around the world to try to catch a glimpse of the mysterious Loch Ness Monster, known as Nessie. There have been lots of sightings of Nessie. Many people believe that Nessie is a prehistoric creature who got trapped in the loch when it was cut off from the sea.

THE CITIES OF SCOTLAND

A COUNTRY OF ITS OWN

Scotland is the last of the countries in the UK that make up our journey. The lowlands of Scotland have beautiful rolling hills and farmland that change into huge mountain ranges and deep <u>glens</u>.

VISITING THE CITIES

As we travelled through Scotland, we heard lots of different accents. We travelled to Edinburgh and Glasgow and then up into the Highlands to Inverness. All those cities were amazing and different.

Dad made me try haggis, the national dish of Scotland. It is made from minced sheep's heart, liver and lungs with onion, oatmeal and other ingredients. It was better than I thought it would be.

THE JOURNEY

Look at all the places we visited on our journey.

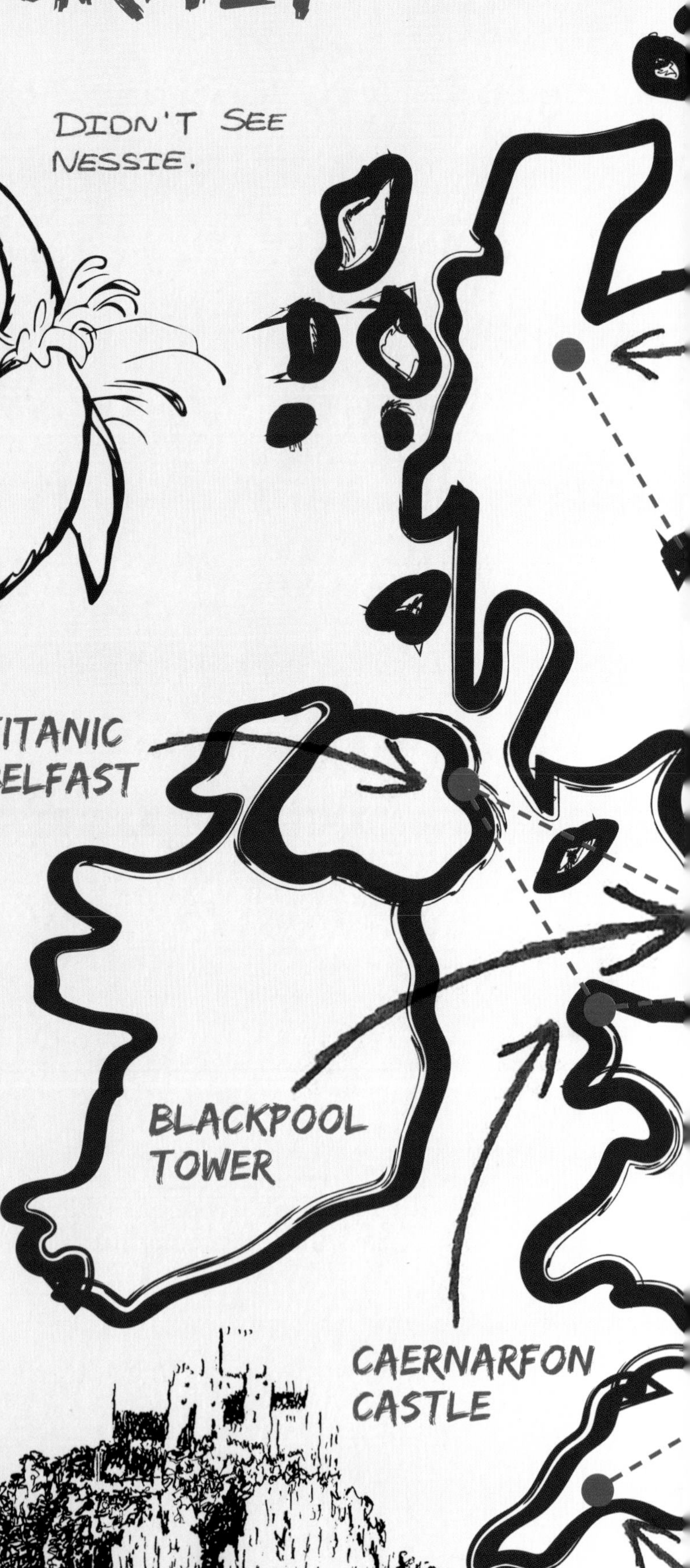

DIDN'T SEE NESSIE.

TITANIC BELFAST

BLACKPOOL TOWER

THERE BE DRAGONS!

CAERNARFON CASTLE

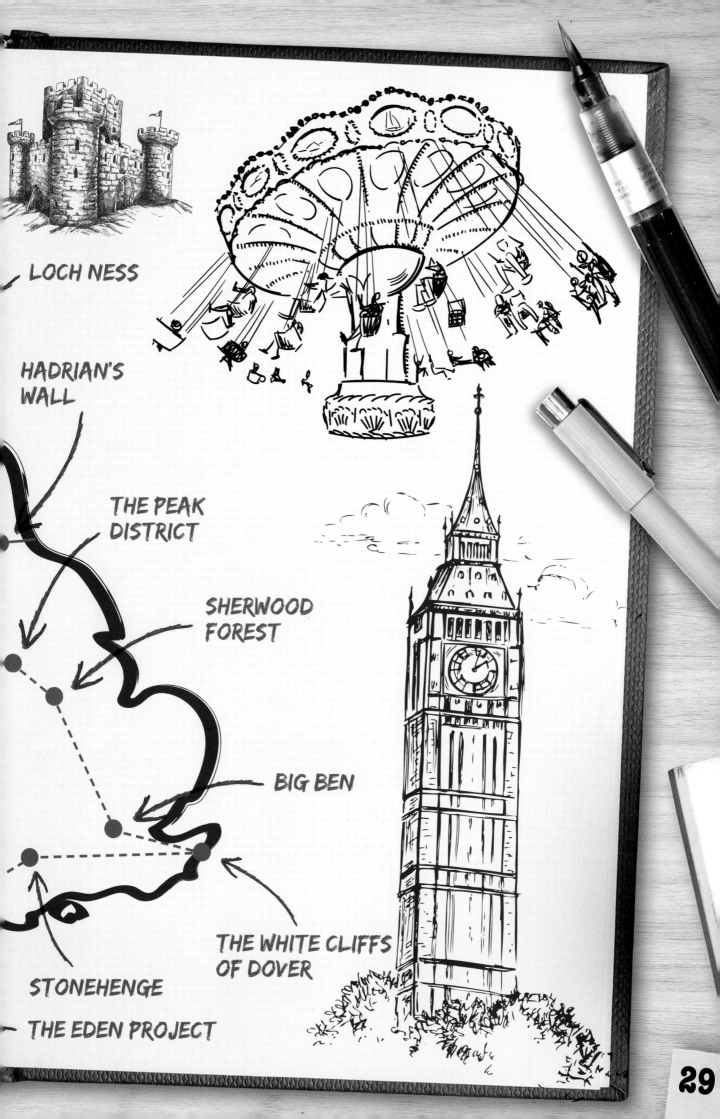

LOCH NESS

HADRIAN'S WALL

THE PEAK DISTRICT

SHERWOOD FOREST

BIG BEN

THE WHITE CLIFFS OF DOVER

STONEHENGE

THE EDEN PROJECT

GOODBYE

I had a great time travelling across the UK. There is so much to see. I loved visiting the castles and trying the local foods. It is amazing how different one county can be from the next.

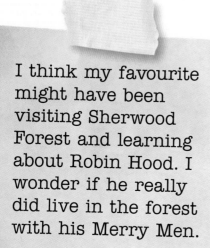

I think my favourite might have been visiting Sherwood Forest and learning about Robin Hood. I wonder if he really did live in the forest with his Merry Men.

GLOSSARY

AD	after the birth of Jesus, which is used as the starting point for many calendars around the world
algae	plants or plant-like living things that have no roots, stems, leaves or flowers
ancestors	people from whom one is descended, for example a great-grandparent
ancient	belonging to the very distant past
Anglo-Saxon	the group of people who lived in England before the Normans arrived
barracks	buildings that soldiers live in
biome	a natural area, home to a community of plants and animals
choirs	groups of people that sing together
conquered	to have taken control of something by force
culture	the way of life and traditions of a group of people
currency	the type of money used in a particular country
Equator	the imaginary line around the Earth that is an equal distance from the North and South Poles
folklore	the traditional culture of a group of people that is passed on by word of mouth
glens	narrow, secluded valleys
hectares	units of area that are equal to 10,000 square-meters
hexagonal	to do with being six-sided
holographic	an image or object made entirely from light
hot springs	areas where water is heated naturally by volcanic heat underground
Industrial Revolution	a period of time from the late 1700s to the early 1800s when technology changed how things were made
pilgrimages	long trips undertaken for religious purposes
prehistoric	before recorded history
rainforest	a forest that gets a lot of rainfall
rural	relating to or characteristic of the countryside
summer solstice	the longest day of the year often celebrated by religions

INDEX